-58

Kill The Lawyers!

D0700887

ISBN 0-9624499-1-1

Library of Congress Catalog Card Number 90-061229

Published by

Prickly Pear Press

Post Office Box 42, Payson, AZ 85547.

Printed by Reliable Reproductions

Design & Illustrations by W. Randall Irvine
Randy's Art Works!

Typography by Deirdre A. Irvine
Great Characters!

Dedicated to Lewis Steiger,
who didn't like lawyers,

And to Reba K. Steiger,
who loved everybody.

Sam the Football Player

Kill The Lawyers!

By Sam Steiger

With A Minimal Apology
By Don Dedera

Prickly Pear Press

Post Office Box 42, Payson, AZ 85547.

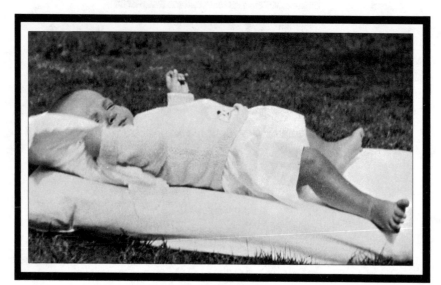

Sam the Manhattanite

Contents

Sam the Sailor on Long Island Sound

Sam on Sam,
a Preface

Probably it was transmitted to me from my Dad. That is not a verifiable certainty, but it will have to do. Seldom did he speak to me; so then when he spoke, I listened. He impressed upon me his Rules of Life, three in number. Never go into a retail business. Never take a partner. And never, ever, appear in a courtroom or solicit the advice of an attorney.

There wasn't much obvious rationale for my Old Man's tenets. As far as I ever knew, he experienced no personal disasters as a retailer. By himself, he ran a nationwide clothing wholesale company. He had no partner to rook him. Nor had he an occasion to press or defend a lawsuit.

In those formative years my very caring Jewish mother wanted me to become either a doctor or a lawyer. Preferably, a doctor. I vividly recall rejecting both career paths. Doctor, because it seemed to promise a stultifyingly dull routine. Lawyer, because even to a boy it seemed unsavory to derive a living from the miseries of people. And the very thought of hanging out with the lawyers' sons known to me, boggled the mind.

I think that readers of this book should understand that my viceral animosity toward the legal profession took root within me that early, and that it grew with every passing year. Based upon observation I came to believe that the majority of society's ills might be eased or cured by the outright elimination of the legal establishment. Or, more practically, diminishing the now pervasive intrusion of legal considerations into every aspect of our culture.

My first grownup encounter with chicanery in the legal arena occurred at Fort Hood, Texas. A newly commissioned second lieutenant, my primary job was command of a tank company platoon. The venerable military system which made truck drivers of Cordon Bleu chefs, and mess sergeants of Teamsters Union gearjammers, worked its wonder with me. Perhaps on the strength of my college major in animal husbandry, I was given the additional duty of company defense attorney, dealing with Article 15 violations. That would be, minor misdemeanors. As new officers are inclined, I took all my assignments seriously; thus, my mind became fully involved when I was called to represent my first defendant in a lawyer-dominated world.

The accused had overstayed a leave because of the terminal illness of his mother. Through correspondence and telephone calls I verified that this young man's mother was dying during his absence—indeed, had since died. My brief in his behalf included a doctor's written statement, a death certificate and a record of the company clerk's telephone log certifying that my client had called to account for his tardiness. Out of my own pocket I bought the soldier a haircut and had his Class A uniform cleaned and pressed. From his platoon sergeant I obtained a sworn statement that he was a splendid soldier, and that the sergeant would be glad to have him back. I acquired character testimonials from his officers school instructors, and from our company commander.

On the day set for trial we were summoned to a pretrial conference with the prosecutor from the judge advocate general's office and the court judges: three battalion commanders. If found guilty my defendant could be reduced to the rank of private, sentenced to time in the stockade and thereafter shipped directly to combat as an infantry rifleman. As a permanent entry in this young man's personnel record, this could potentially downgrade the type of his discharge, and shadow the rest of his life. So, deeply concerned and convinced of his innocence, I began to explain the circumstances.

The prosecutor cut me off short. The presiding officer looked at his watch and said, "Let's go hang this guilty bastard." And they did.

During my own time in Korea, some fourteen months on the front line, being shot at and even hit, I never saw a lawyer at any level of command below division. I certainly never saw the prosecutor who conspired to severely punish an innocent lad with duty in the trenches. In fact, military law more likely was practiced in the relative comfort and absolute safety of Japan. My disdain for the calling intensified.

Not long after my return to the civilian world, to the role of rancher near Prescott, Arizona, I annually conducted a very successful horse auction. We'd usually sell more than a hundred head for a great deal of money.

One year a particular buyer was also a seller. He paid for his purchases by check, which bounced. So I common-sensibly deducted an appropriate amount from monies due him from his sold horses. Six months later he sued.

In the belief that the case was clear cut, I decided to represent myself. I researched the statutes, prepared a brief, cited relevant cases and presented the case in an opening statement. The superior court judge ruled that no trial was necessary. He summarily declared in favor of the plaintiff, and that was that.

Soon afterward, still furious, I sought out the judge, who happened to be a friend of mine. I asked how possibly a defendant could lose such a case.

"Sam," he replied, "of course you were had. Lawyers don't appreciate laymen playing in their playpen." My estimation of the system took another drop.

During my tenure as a state senator and five terms in the U.S. House of Representatives I had the opportunity, nay, the necessity, to come to know a great many lawyers far better than I wanted to. There were then, as are now, more lawyers than people in both chambers of Congress. The so-called agency congressional liaison individuals (actually lobbiests for federal bureaus) were and are nearly all lawyers.

Clearly, there are differences among lawyers. I have met many who were courteous, intelligent, competent, honest and diligent. As often as not they were the older generation, including some who read the law rather than attended some legal instructional facility. These senior practitioners are almost human. They don't take unethical advantage, seek unreasonable conditions or bend the truth.

But something seemingly happens to many of the younger attorneys, maybe as early as law school. They now are viewed as having such widely differing standards from the rest of us, they generally are reduced to socializing with their own. They lunch at their own tables, drink in their own bars, join together in their own clubs, camp out in their own tents and lionize one another at their own banquets. I am acquainted with lay parents who dissuade their children from disporting with lawyers, lest they become grandparents of babies borne or sired by lawyers.

And more. I know surgeons who turn away lawyer patients out of fear of litigation. Yet more. Hunting guides shun them. Non-lawyer golfers avoid their company. Is the day far off when lawyers will be excluded from membership in clubs and congregations? Yet the legions of lawyers grow by the hour.

Meanwhile, in the motherland of Great Britain, from whose body of English common law the American system sprang, the number of practicing attorneys is controlled. Ergo: fewer lawyers, fewer lawsuits. While it may take two years or more for a suit to reach an American court, actions routinely reach courts within sixty days in any jurisdiction in Britain. The British system is just and concise, and is driven by innate human greed. For, in Great Britain when a plaintiff loses a civil suit, the plaintiff pays the defense legal fees. Thus, lawsuits generally are limited to actions of merit.

By adopting the British method, we can starve out at least half of the current overabundance of American lawyers. We may run the risk of more failed lawyers running for public office and seeking seats on the bench, but the worthwhile trade-off will be the beginning of the restoration of the health of the republic. The young people of our once-great nation will have a brighter future.

No longer should we abide a legal system in which normal social activities are spoiled, and foolish deeds are rewarded. It is ridiculous that public events which once benefitted charities are now canceled because of the high cost of liability insurance. Family doctors are withholding maternity care, leaving that practice to specialists burdened by excessive insurance costs. Obstetricians simply will not practice in small towns where they would be most vulnerable to the vagaries of pregnancy, childbirth and infant mortality. The end is in sight for contact sports in small, poor schools with no budgets for insurance. Our culture is crumbling.

Our coddling of culprits is a national disgrace. Our disdain of the rights of victims is reprehensible. A bank robber flees with a money bag, which explodes and injures him. He sues the bank and wins a large settlement. A dipsomaniacal woman drinks a fifth of bourbon every day for twelve years and develops cirrhosis of the liver. She sues the whisky company. She wins. A drunk pilot crashes an airplane. He sues the aircraft manufacturer. He loses, but because it cost $2 million to defend the lawsuit, the manufacturer ceases to build general aviation planes. More culture crumbles.

There is a good deal already wrong with our civilization—undersupported schools, drug use, erosion of individual responsibility, miscrepancy in high office, corruption in low office, afternoon television, well done steaks, professional wrestling, unabashed pimping and political reporting. But the most glaring evil abroad in the land today is the practice of law by armies of avaricious attorneys.

They must be stopped. Scorn will help.

Thus, this book.

⚖

Sam the High School Student

I. Lawyers as People

Benjamin Frankin is supposed to have penned the epitaph:
God works wonders, now and then;
Behold! a lawyer, an honest man.
And when it was put upon a headstone, a citizen commented, "Imagine that. They've gone and buried two men in the same grave."

⚖

A lawyer, an avid golfer, was pursuing a solo round at his country club.

He played well until shanking his approach toward the seventh green. As he flailed away in a bunker, he grumbled, "Damn, I'd give anything to have a million dollars in the bank and shoot scratch golf."

With that, the devil appeared, and said, "You will never have less than $1 million in your checking account, and you will shoot lower than par. All I want in exchange is your soul."

The lawyer thought about that, and demanded, "What's the catch?"

According to John J. Low

⚖

He can compress the fewest ideas in the most words of any man I ever met.

Abraham Lincoln, referring to a prominent lawyer

⚖

Almost all lawyers have delusions of adequacy that transend their level of competence.

Thought While Painting a Crosswalk

1

I am not a lawyer, and shall always strive to live a good and honest life, so as not to become one.

Steiger's Promise

⚖

Some lawyers are so popular that when they die, people are eager to buy pieces of the rope.

The Author's Collection

⚖

Two balloonists became disoriented when a dense fog engulfed them as they passed over a vast forest. After some hours of floating aloft, the balloon entered a hole in the fog, directly above a clearing in the forest.

"Where...are..we?" shouted one of the aviators.

"You...are...in...a...balloon!" yelled back the man on the ground.

"Goddam lawyers," hissed one balloonist to the other.

"How do you know that guy is a lawyer?"

"Well, analyze what he said. First, his statement was accurate. Second, his speech was quite precise. And the information was utterly useless."

As told by Wally Perry

⚖

As one gets older, litigation replaces sex.

Gore Vidal

⚖

What's the difference between a woman lawyer and a pit bulldog? Lip gloss.

Found by Steiger on police blotter

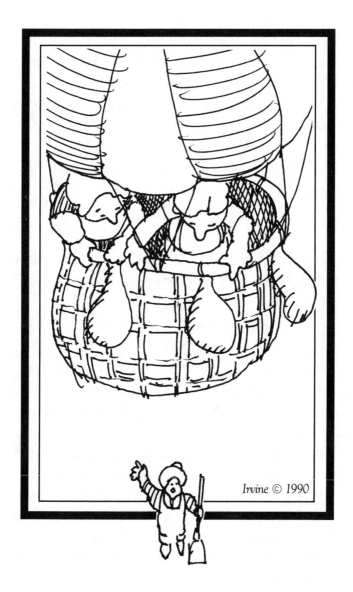

Irvine © 1990

Old English epitaph for a lawyer:

Beneath this smooth stone by the bone of his bone
Sleeps Master John Gill;
By lies when alive this attorney did thrive,
And now that he's dead, he lies still.

☥☥

I think we may class lawyers in the natural history of monsters.

John Keats

☥☥

When a lawyer falls into the raging Colorado River, that's a misfortune. When somebody pulls him out, that's a calamity.

From the Rewritten Boy Scout Handbook by S.S.

☥☥

A light airplane en route to a religious conference crashed, killing the occupants, a minister, a rabbi and a priest. A lawyer on the ground was fatally struck by the falling craft.

So the four men arrived in heaven simultaneously. St. Peter directed the minister to a tiny basement apartment, the rabbi to a fourth floor walkup and the priest to a solitary cell. The lawyer was handed the key to a lavishly appointed thirty-room manor house.

"When those honorable clergymen were given so little, why so much for me?" asked the lawyer.

"Since the beginning of time," explained St. Pete, "you're the first lawyer we ever had."

As told by Budge Ruffner

☥☥

Every once in a while you meet a fellow in some honorable walk of life that was once admitted to the bar.

Frank McKinney Hubbard

Lawyers are selfmade, and they worship their creator.

Theology 101, Prof. Steiger

Satan and the Lord fell into a serious argument over the maintenance of the fence dividing Heaven and Hell.

Finally, in exasperation the Lord threatened to sue. "Oh, yeah," smirked The Evil One. "And on your side of the fence where do you think you'll find a lawyer?"

The Author's Collection

It is a feature of nearly every Utopia, that there has been no place in it for lawyers.

Benjamin Cardozo

No lawyer's shirt is too young to be stuffed.

Sam, the Taxidermist

Three surgeons were discussing the merits of various professions as patients. One said he preferred to operate on engineers because they were so orderly, all the organs were exactly in the right places. The second doctor expressed a bias toward artists because they were so expressive, everything was color-coded.

"I'd rather work on lawyers, because they are so

simple," said the third doctor. "There are only two organs, the face and the backside—and they are interchangeable."

⚖

Epitaph for the lawyer Sir John Strange:
Here lies an honest lawyer,
And that is Strange.

⚖

Two blind animals bumped into one another in the woods.

"What are you?"

"I don't know...what are you?"

"I don't know either."

So they agreed to feel each other all over and figure it out.

Said one, "You have long ears, soft fur, and a stubby tail. You must be a bunny rabbit."

It was then the rabbit's turn. "You're slick and slithery. You have little beady eyes and a pointy head. Your tongue flicks in and out. You must be a lawyer!"

⚖

Imagine a remote village in darkest Africa, and an establishment named The Cannibal Cafe. Diners are protesting one price on the menu.

Roast missionary is $10, reasonable enough. Boiled archaeologist just $12. And broiled white hunter only $14.

But whole, dressed lawyer is listed at $140. Explains the chef: "Did you ever have to *clean* one of those things?"

Irvine © 1990

Law school prepares people to strut while sitting down.

Physiology 101, Prof. Steiger

⚖

A lawyer is a person who is invited to all the best places—once.

The Author's Collection

⚖

A man passing a cemetery noticed an extraordinarily deep, open grave.

"'It's for a lawyer," explained the grave digger. "We bury them 15 feet under, because deep down, they're good guys."

The Author's Collection

⚖

A lawyer is a person who knows the price of everything and the value of nothing.

Lewis Steiger's Constant

⚖

I wish I were as cocksure of anything, as lawyers are of everything.

The Author's Philosophy

⚖

How do you tell the difference between a dead skunk and a dead lawyer lying in the road? There are skid marks in front of the skunk.

The Author's Collection

⚖

If the laws could speak for themselves, they would complain of the lawyers in the first place.

Lord Halifax

⚖

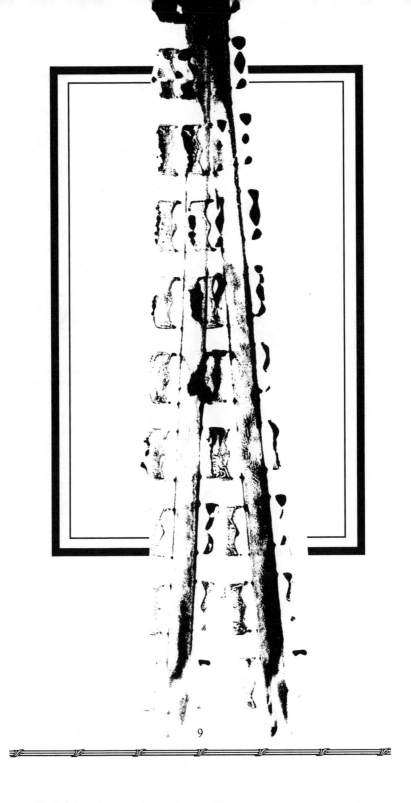

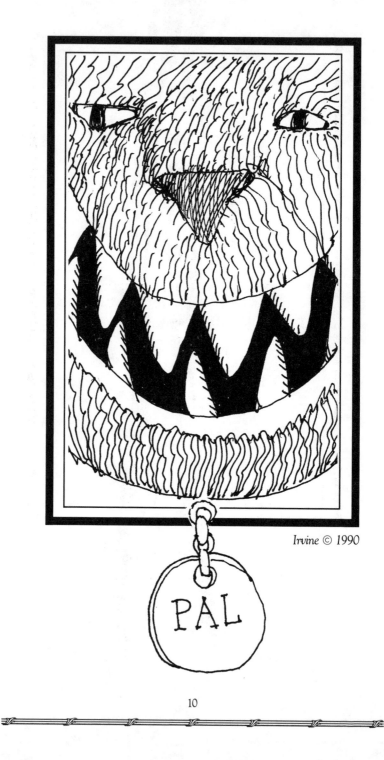

Irvine © 1990

Why are 200 lawyers buried in sand up to their necks? Not enough sand.

The Author's Collection

☙⚖❧

What is black and brown and looks good on a lawyer? A Doberman pinscher.

The Author's Collection

☙⚖❧

A stranger arrived in a town just as a funeral procession was passing by.

Behind the hearse marched a man who held on a leash a large, snarling dog with dagger-like fangs. And behind the man and dog followed 70 people, in single file.

"What's the story?" asked the stranger.

"That's my lawyer, in the hearse," said the man. "This is the dog that bit him to death."

Pause.

"Uh," whispered the stranger. "Could I borrow that dog?"

"Sure," said the dog owner. "Get in line...."

Adapted from Henny Youngman

☙⚖❧

What do you get when you cross a lawyer with a streetwalker? An offer you cannot understand.

Downs Matthews

☙⚖❧

LAWYERS: Where do they come from?

The Evolution of
LAWYERUS SHYSTERUS AMERICANUS

By Leslie S. Collins & Irving Schulman

Introduction:

At last count there were 527,000 attorneys in America. Many Americans believe ravenous lawyers, like an African locust plague, have intruded into practically every aspect of our lives. It is true, however, that just as it is now almost impossible for an owner to maintain and fix the modern automobile, so too the complexity of our affairs and the aggressiveness of our fellows requires societal navigators and bodyguards. Enter the lawyer.

The evolution of the modern attorney, "Lawyerus shyterus (lawyer'us shy ster'us,)" can be traced back to the fifth century BC. Although law codes and law suits were recorded more than 3500 years ago, humanity seemed to have gotten along fine without the benefit of counsel until approximately 500 BC. Plaintiff and defendant pleaded their own cases before a priest, elder, mayor, or ruler who then rendered a judgment.

The Greek Period

About 500 BC, a bright litigant hit on the idea of taking lessons in oratory to improve his odds of winning. He must have been quite successful because schools of oratory sprang up quickly. The professors of those school were actually a primitive ancestor of today's trial lawyers known as *rhetores* or professor of oratory. As we all know, successful trial advocacy often turns on style over substance. But sometimes content and substance can be important, and so it was in ancient Greece. The *logographi* or speech writer was the first in a long line of legal ghost writer, an early version of today's English solicitor or American law clerk.

They did not resemble "Lawyerus shysterus," however. The litigant, in general, still had to represent himself. The only exception was found in the kin group. The head of a kin group (clan or extended family) had an obligation to speak on behalf of a defendant.

Around the same time, a sort of advocate — probably a "mutant" rhetores — called a *synegoros* appeared. The synegoros, on rare occasions, was appointed by the court or tribunal to assist a litigant or supplement another's exposition of a case. A synegoros might assist cities, public bodies, or individuals, (accused or accuser). When he represented a city with regard to proposed legislation, the synegoros functioned as a primitive city attorney.

The Roman Period

Researchers excavating the archives of Italian libraries have found the remains of interesting and long extinct creatures *juris prudentes* — wise men of the law. (The gene for wiseness was somehow lost in the evolutionary process.) While not yet Lawyerus shysterus, this early Roman species spent his adult life, studying and debating the law. Over the centuries, juris prudentes engaged in discussions, opinions and debates which accumulated into a body of law. But he did not practice law; he seldom took cases and when he did, accepted no fees.

During the first century BC, a species known as *advocati* evolved from the juris prudentes. The advocati proved expert advice to those involved in lawsuits but did not represent them. However, by the second century AD, the advocati were permitted to speak on behalf of their clients under some circumstances. As those "circumstances" became more and more frequent, due no doubt to the skill of the advocate in swaying the court to find in favor of his client, he became known as a *causidici* or "speaker of cases." Here, at last was a true ancestor of today's "Lawyerus shysterus."

One interesting peculiarity of the Roman system which is now extinct, was its unusual concept of principal—agent. The advocate of the litigant was not viewed as an agent. Instead, the advocate became the litigant himself. If one individual sued another through advocates, the court could order the attorney of one to pay the attorney of the other. Unfortunately, this strong incentive for lawyers to be diligent in presenting their cases, or pay the penalty, quickly came into disfavor. Perhaps if this structure were revived, America's litigation plague could be healed.

The causidi species gradually evolved into two subspecies known as *cognitors* and *procurators* both of whom were representatives for ligitations who appeared in place of the litigant, especially in Roman provinces.

They were differentiated only by the methods of their appointment. Cognitors were appointed by the client in a formal way using a set form of words, while the procurator was hired through an informal agreement ("You want the job, you got it").

Little attempt was made to assure the competency of the cognitor or procurator. Edicts were issued forbidding minors, the deaf, the blind, women, and other "ne'er-do-wells" to represent others. There was, however, no standard for training or level of legal knowledge required to become an advocate. As the charging of fees for legal advice was considered next to immoral, only the wealthy could afford to study or "practice" law. Compensation took the form of recognition for the socially and politically ambitious.

As in today's courtroom, Roman court "justice" relied heavily on the oratorical and theatrical skills. Following cognitors, and procurators, *patronus causarum*, and the causidici, evolved. The patronus causarum served both as jurisconsult, or advisor, and advocate, or trial lawyer. Both plaintiff and defendant required at least four patronus causaum to present a "respectable" case. These advocates orchestrated a presentation which included irrelevant rhetoric, dressing the accused for the part and bringing in swarms of relatives dressed in mourning (all techniques still in use today). Claques were hired to applaud the advocates' speeches. But though they acted like true "Lawyerus shysterus", the patronus causarum lacked two "essential" elements: formal education and remuneration for services.

With the founding of the empire, the old monied class, who did not need remuneration, no longer engaged in law as a hobby and political office no longer depended on popular election. As early as the reign of Claudis (41-54 AD) the maximum fee of 10,000 sesterces (a sesterces was originally worth two and one-half asses, but by this time 10,000 sesterces was worth about $475) was fixed by law. Advocates were subject to prosecution if they accepted more. Today, however, a true "shysterus" would never agree to fixed maximum fees; further, he would have no need for two and one-half asses, (the more cynical would say) because he is one.

By the fifth century AD, a nearly perfect "Lawyerus shysterus" appeared. He was educated in a school of law and his numbers were limited. In 468 a statute prohibited the practice of advocacy by those not admitted to practice. Presumably of even more importance to "Lawyerus shysterus", he was allowed to collect fees for his services.

During the Roman period, much of the foundation for the modern legal profession was laid. The nature of the "Lawyerus shysterus," his professional behavior and acceptance to practice were all concepts very similiar to today's. Gradually, a science of law was developing with jurist-made law a key ingredient.

The Dark Ages

Roman law lingered in Euope until about the seventh or eighth Century AD. Because literacy was limited to the church, so was the practice of law.

"Lawyerus shysterus" soon became a cleric specializing in both canon and common law. But in 1219 clerics were prohibited by Rome from practicing common law and "Lawyerus" (who was never comfortable in the role anyway) put away his cleric robes forever.

With the Renaissance in 1420 came a surge of interest in classical Rome and its achievements. Extensive study was made of Roman law with consideration of its relevance to contemporary life. France and Italy, in particular, accepted much Roman law into their civil systems. As in Rome "Lawyerus shysterus" reemerged and gained respect.

England

While "Lawyerus shysterus" survived relatively intact in France and Italy, he split into two distinct subspecies in England. Both of these subspecies evolved from a common ancestor know as *sergeants-at-law* which emerged in the period between 1250 to 1350. Sergeants-at-large practiced common law exclusively in the court of common pleas. They surrounded themselves with underlings and apprentices at law and congregated in areas near the courts forming "Inns of Court" or little colonies. This permitted them to share facilities such as libraries and offices, make themselves more accessible to their clients, and gave them the opportunity to exchange experiences and discuss the law.

But as work loads increased, apprentices were divided into "pleaders" who appeared in court to present pleas and "attorneys" who were more legal advisors. The pleaders became today's barristers who try all cases, and from their ranks come England's judges. (By 1600, only the barristers had the right to practice before the courts.) The attorneys became today's solicitors, whose function today is primarily general legal advice and documentation, as opposed to trial work. Etiquette went so far as to prohibit social contact between barristers and solicitors.

Though social contact is no longer prohibited, the system of barristers and solicitors having separate functions remains. Clients go to solicitors, solicitors prepare their cases and then go to barristers who present the case in court. This system allows relatively few barristers (approx. 4800) to handle all of the trial work in England. This separation is seen as a strength in keeping the legal profession in England self-regulating and independent. Although solicitors form partnerships and large firms, barristers are forbidden from doing so. They must work as individuals and may not be employees of firms or interest groups and still practice before the bench.

Summation

America, as British colony, developed its legal system from the common law of England. Early on, however, wigs amd costumes were shed and the distinction between solicitor and barrister was abandoned. Shorn of all vestiges of Roman wisdom, English decorum and propriety, today the American lawyer can hustle business on TV, chase ambulances, pull cases out of thin air, and gin up fees in the true spirit of American free enterprise. ENTER *Lawyerus shysterus americanus.*

Today's lawyer has passed through many phases in the evolutionary process. He began as a professor of oratory and speech writer, evolved into an advisor and finally to his present role. What is that role? Defender of the poor, pawn of the rich, seeker of truth and justice, mad dog. Take your pick.

Leslie Collins is land sales coordinator and Irving Schulman is a research specialist for The Pensus Group. Printed with permission.

Sam the Candidate

II. Lawyers as Practitioners

A lawyer died unexpectedly, and appeared at Heaven's gate where St. Peter was faithfully keeping accounts.

"This is an outrage!" thundered the attorney. "I'm much too young to die...I'm only 33 years old."

"We have your age as 98."

"What kind of arithmetic arrived at that incorrect number?"

Said St. Peter, "We added up your billable hours."

♎

There are many towns that are too small for even one lawyer to sustain himself practicing the law. There is no town too small for two lawyers to make a living.

The Author's Collection

♎

Lawful, adj. Compatible with the will of a judge having jurisdiction.

Ambrose Bierce

♎

Law is a bottomless pit.

The History of John Bull, 1712

♎

"How's Lawyer Jones, Doctor?"

"He lies at death's door."

"Now that is real determination. At death's door, and still lying."

The Author's Collection

♎

Where there's a will, there's a lawsuit.

⚖

If you laid all our laws end to end, there would be no end.

⚖

I heartily accept the motto, "That government is best which governs least"; and I should like to see it acted up to more rapidly and systematically. Carried out, it finally amounts to this, which I also believe— "That government is best which governs not at all"; and when men are prepared for it, that will be the kind of government which they will have. Government is best but an expedient; but most governments are sometimes, inexpedient.

● ● ●

We should be men first, and subjects afterward. It is not desirable to cultivate a respect for the law, so much as for the right.

⚖

Most lawyers who win a case advise their clients that, "We have won," and when justice has frowned upon their cause that, "You have lost."

⚖

A receiver is appointed by the court to take what's left.

⚖

Lawyers earn a living by the sweat of their browbeating.

James Gibbons Huneker

⚖

Innocence, n. The state or condition of a criminal whose counsel has fixed the jury.

Ambrose Bierce

⚖

A story is told of Sir Henry Irving, the imminent actor, who had been a witness in a street robbery. The defendant's lawyer demanded to know what time the alleged theft occurred.

"I think...," began Sir Henry.

Sarcastically, the lawyer broke in, "I don't want to know what you think. Tell me what you know."

"You don't want to know what I think?"

"No!" yelled the lawyer.

"Then I might as well step down," said Sir Henry. "I can't talk without thinking. I am not a lawyer."

Quoted by Don Dedera

⚖

Many lawyers are modest, and all lawyers have much to be modest about.

Steiger's Fourteenth Postulation

⚖

Ignorance of the law excuses no man—from practicing it.

Addison Mizner

⚖

Lawyer, n. One skilled in circumvention of the law.

Ambrose Bierce

⚖

There was a young lawyer named Rex
Who was sadly deficient in sex.
Arraigned for exposure
He said with composure,
"De minimus non curat lex." *

* *"The law is not concerned with trifles."*

⚖

What is it that a duck cannot, a goose can, and a lawyer should? Shove its bill...well....

Overheard at Court

⚖

One listens to one's lawyer prattle on as long as one can stand it and then signs where indicated.

Alexander Woollcott

⚖

Lawyer: one who protects us against robbery by taking away the temptation.

H.L. Mencken

⚖

Tree, n. A tall vegetable intended by nature to serve as a penal apparatus, though through a miscarriage of justice most trees bear only a negligible fruit, or none at all....

Ambrose Bierce

⚖

Accuracy and diligence are much more necessary to a lawyer than great comprehension of mind; or brilliancy of talent. His business is to refine, define, split hairs, look into authorities, and compare cases. A man can never gallop over the fields of law on Pegasus, nor fly across them on the wings of oratory. If he would stand on *terra firma*, he must descend. If he would be a great lawyer, he must first consent to become a great drudge.

Daniel Webster

It is the trade of lawyers to question everything, yield nothing, and talk by the hour.

Holbrook Jackson or *Thomas Jefferson*

The law (is) a horrible business.
There is no such thing as justice—in or out of court.

Clarence S. Darrow, (1857-1938) American criminal lawyer, writer

Any law written with more than fifty words contains at least one loophole.

Anonymous

Probably all laws are useless; for good men do not want laws at all, and bad men are made no better by them.

Demonax, c. A.D. 150.

Law is an institution of the most pernicious tendency. The instituion once begun, can never be brought to a close. No action of any man was ever the same as any other action, had ever the same degree of utility or injury. As new cases occur, the law is perpetually found deficient. It is therefore perpetually necessary to make new laws. The volume in which justice records her prescriptions is forever increasing, and the world would not contain the books that might be written. The consequences of the infinitude of law is its uncertainty. Law was made that a plain man might know what he had to expect, and yet the most skillful practitioners know nothing about the event of my suit.

William Godwin

A precedent embalms a principle.

From a speech, House of Commons, 1848, by Benjamin Disraeli, 1804-1881, English statesman, novelist, poet

The lawyers make th' law, th' judges make th' errors, but th' iditors make th' juries.

American Magazine, October, 1906, Finley Peter Dunne, "Mister Dooley," 1867-1936, American satirist

If you can eat sawdust without butter, you can be a success in the law.

Oliver Wendell Holmes

Written laws are like spiders' webs, and will like them only entangle and hold the poor and weak, while the rich and powerful will easily break through them.

Anacharis, c. 600 B.C., Sythian philosopher to Solon

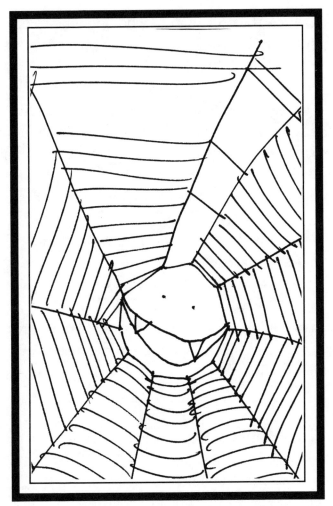

Irvine © 1990

Lawyer: the only man in whom ignorance of the law is not punished.

Elbert Hubbard

⚖

Gravely ill, an English lawyer constructed his own will, leaving all of his estate to "fools and madmen." He explained, "From such, I had it, and to such I give it again."

Letter from London

⚖

The United States is the greatest law factory the world has ever known.

Charles Evans Hughes

⚖

It is hard to say whether doctors of law or divinity have made the greater advances in the lucrative business of mystery.

Edmund Burke

⚖

"For a man who has reached such a terrible place in life," sneered the prosecutor toward the defendant, "you seem to be fairly intelligent."

"I'm under oath," cooed the defendant. "I can't return the compliment."

The Author's Collection

⚖

Barrister, n. One of ten thousand varieties of the genus Lawyer. In England the functions of a barrister are distinct from those of a solicitor. The one advises, the other executes; but the thing advised and the thing executed is the client.*

Ambrose Bierce

*One more time, perhaps, it is worth recalling Dorothy Parker's explanation of how she spent a holiday in England: "Sliding down barristers."

Editor.

⚖

Notes from a law school lecture:

"If you have the facts on your side, hammer them into the jury. If you have the law on your side, hammer it into the judge."

And what if you have no advantage of facts or law? "Hammer the table!"

⚖

Jury, n. A number of persons appointed by a court to assist the attorneys in preventing law from degenerating into justice.

Ambrose Bierce

⚖

When a lawyer does something he perceives he should be ashamed of, he says it is his duty, and laymen would not understand.

Sam's Rule of Thumb

⚖

Irvine © 1990

A Jew, a Hindu and a lawyer were traveling together when their car broke down on a lonely road. They asked to spend the night at a nearby farm house.

The farmer explained that he had only two extra beds; one man would have to sleep in the barn. The Jew volunteered, but soon was knocking at the back door of the farmhouse.

"There is pig in the barn," he said, "and my religion does not allow me to associate with an unclean animal."

The Hindu then went to the barn. But he, too, soon was knocking at the door. He said his religion forbade him from occupying the same space as a holy cow.

So then the lawyer went to the barn. And soon, a knocking at the back door. It was the pig and cow.

⚖

Lawyers *never* vacation on the coast. They're afraid stray cats will bury them in the sand.

Mailed in from San Diego

⚖

The Devil,
Them Lawyers
and Ol' Sam's Steers
by Vance Wampler

The Devil sent his riders out
To rustle him some steers
He had a yen fer barbecue
And had fer several years

Now, cattle rustlers down below
Work on the Devil's spread
They used to be them lawyer types
Before they wound up dead

Them crooked sneaky lawyer pokes
The Devil loved them boys
They's trained to lie and cheat and steal
It's what they most enjoys

And lawyer gals he keeps as pets
They keep his ol' horns clean
Wire brush his coat and pointy tail
And other things obscene

But, Hell it is a-fillin' up
With millions more each day
Them lawyers they keep comin' down
From every which-away

The Devil keeps some from the fire
When they bring down a writ
And promise they do anythin'
If Devil's work is it

A-course they all kin qualify
They beg on mercy's grounds
He keeps the worst cooks up the rest
As food fer his ol' hounds

Them rustlers dressed in black they was
In robes like judges wear
A-ridin' fast their evil broncs
Through Arizona there

The Devil told 'em where to go
"Find Sam's ol' cattle spread
Up in them brushy Prescott hills
His steers has been well fed"

Them rustler pokes in flowin' robes
A-flappin' in the breeze
They're ridin' hard and purty soon
A small ranch house they sees

And rein up and then swarm around
That cowboy's ranchin' place
And keep their eyes peeled fer the sight
Of hisself jest in case

'Cause Devil warned them lawyer boys,
"Avoid that poke fer shore
Jest git his steers and brang 'em back
He's ornery to the core

"That feller he is fearsome tough
Cantankerous you'll find
He don't let loose he gits a-holt
Won't take no nevermind"

Now, Sam he sees them lawyer boys
A-sneakin' 'round his house
And figures it's more government
Come out to count his cows

He gits his rope and rides 'em down
Ties up them lawyers well
And snugs 'em to a catclaw tree
And listens to 'em yell

Them wild-eyed cowards they is scairt
They howl and show their fears
Whilest Sam he gits his Barlow out
He's a-gonna make some steers

Imagine then to his surprise
He finds what lawyers lacks
He opens up jest empty bags
Ain't nothin' in them sacks

"Habeus Juevos," ol' Sam says
"I truly ain't surprised
You lawyers had me scairt one time
Until I realized

"You mostly do the Devil's work
Real men ain't fit fer that"
He cut 'em free, them sorry pokes
And chased 'em with his hat

"You tell yer boss I don't waste time
On them who ain't a man
He wants to deal with this ol' boy
He kin ketch me if he can

"Go git on back where you belong
You sorry rustler crew
You tell yer boss he wants my steers
I'll trade him them fer you

"Don't send no politicians up
They's all yer lyin' kin
And in cahoots with Devil too
And live down where you been

"Don't send no lady lawyers up
If the Devil wants the trade
What you ain't got them darlin's growed
As women, I'm afraid

Irvine © 1990

"And made 'em ugly and as mean
As grizzly bears gone wrong
That Devil he deserves you all
Git back where you belong"
• • •
Well, Sam he was a-feelin' good
He watched 'em makin' dust
Smiled to hisself and said out loud
"Lord ... reckon how You must

"Give folks some problems jest fer fun
'Cause You like good jokes too
You give us cholla cactus, snakes,
And dirty work to do

"You make it rain when it's too wet
And give us drought, it's dry
It makes us strong, them challenges
But, Lord, I ask You why

"You have to bring into our lives
Them Lawyers fer awhile
At least when I been called back home
Fer judgment I kin smile

"You'll hear my case — no lawyers there
And You'll be fair, I know
Without them kind it shore will be
PURE HEAVEN, don't You know."

Sam the Cowboy

III. Lawyers as Parasites

An aged widow in tattered clothing shuffled into a lawyer's office. She had been arrested for vagrancy, and her case was set soon for trial. In a voice frail and quivering the woman explained that she was not a vagrant, but rather a resident in a tiny slum house. She said she eked out a living by retrieving aluminum cans from alley trash cans. As proof, she showed the lawyer a crisp $100 bill she had just received from the recycling salvage yard for a month of scavenging.

"The best thing you can do is plead guilty," advised the attorney, plucking the bill from her fingers.

When she had gone, the lawyer gave the banknote a satisfying little snap. This revealed a second $100 bill, stuck to the first. And it presented to the lawyer an ethical dilemma.

Should he share the money 50-50 with his partner, or pocket it all himself?

The Author's Collection

⚖

The trouble with law and government is lawyers.

Clarence Darrow

⚖

Defendant, n. In law, an obliging person who devotes his time and character to preserving property for his lawyer.

Ambrose Bierce

⚖

The law, in its majestic equality, forbids the rich as well as the poor to sleep under bridges, to beg in the streets and steal bread.

Anatole France
☗☗

Lawyers are capable of committing any crime not requiring courage.

From the Author's Collection
☗☗

A lawyer makes his conscience not his guide, but his accomplice.

Taken from the Sheriff's Log by Sam
☗☗

A priest, a Boy Scout and a lawyer were aloft in an airplane when the engine konked out. There were only two parachutes.

The lawyer grabbed a bundle, shouted that he was the sharpest lawyer in the United States and that his clients desperately needed him. He jumped.

"You have your whole life ahead of you, my son," said the priest, "So you are the one who should save himself."

"No, Father, we will both live." replied the Boy Scout. "The sharpest lawyer in the country just jumped with my knapsack."

☗☗

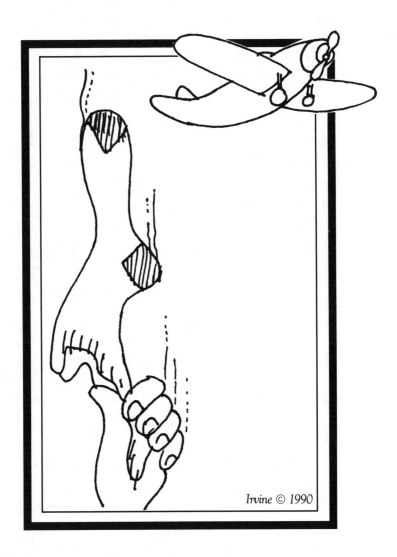

Irvine © 1990

A countryman between two lawyers is like a fish between two cats.

Benjamin Franklin

Why are lawyers the laboratory experimental animal of choice over rats?

Four reasons.

1. There are more of them.
2. They more closely resemble human anatomy.
3. Lab assistants never get emotionally attached to them.
4. There are some things that rats simply refuse to do.

The Author's Collection

A lawyer is a learned gentleman who rescues your estate from your enemies and keeps it himself.

Lord Henry Brougham

Lawsuit: a machine which you go in as a pig and come out as a sausage.

Ambrose Bierce

The law protects everybody who can afford to hire a good lawyer.

Anonymous

I have a solution to the lawyer glut. It is as simple, brilliant and certain as the paper clip. It is this: Let's file a class action suit against the law schools of the nation.

We will charge them with manufacturing a product that has brought this great nation to litigious gridlock. We will cite the schools for rewriting a centuries-old code of ethics that clearly defined right and wrong, that allowed even agnostics to respect the Judea-Christian, "Do unto others as you would have them do unto you...and harm no one," to read, "Harm no one except that it profit thee and me."

We will add to our bill of particulars the charge that the law schools are responsible for the 24-hour billable day. Yes, it is a system that allows members of the profession to charge clients for the hours lawyers sleep (for some individuals, perhaps justified, in that this is when they think best).

We the plaintiffs will not seek financial compensation. No punitive damages. Nay, my friends, we will shut down these schools forever. This will be too late for us, but our children and their children can see a bright tomorrow.

Of course, there will be no shortage of lawyers eager to press our case. Members of the existing bar will realize that with no new lawyers emerging from law schools, competition will be reduced. This will mean accelerating business for surviving lawyers, and higher fees. For a while, greed will keep lawyers in the business of law. Lawyers will forego temptations to run for public office. The quality of government will rise dramatically.

In time, there will be but one lawyer remaining. And he or she will be living at Fort Knox in possession of all the money in America. By then there will be but one law left on the books. The law will stipulate that upon the passing of the last lawyer, his or her estate shall be divided equally among the citizens of the nation.

And peace and prosperity will reign.

Sam Himself

⚖

The late, Watergate hearings Senator Sam Ervin told a story about a lawyer who appeared at a revival meeting. The preacher impulsively asked the attorney to say a prayer. Only momentarily taken aback, the lawyer prayed earnestly, "Stir up much strife amongst the people, Lord, lest thy servant perish."

Memories of Washington

⚖

A golden oldie has two lawyers and a priest afloat in a lifeboat. Day after day they drift, till finally they spy an island. But offshore cruises a school of sharks. Half mad with thirst, one lawyer jumps overboard and swims toward the beach. Amazingly, the sharks part ranks and give the swimmer safe passage.

"It's a miracle," says the priest.

"No," says the other lawyer, "just professional courtesy.

Jack Cavness told it.

⚖

Irvine © 1990

Criminal lawyer, n., in the English language, a commonplace redundancy.

Found inside a Guiness Stout bottle washed up on Tempe Beach.

At last: A lawyer you can bite, chew, swallow or spit out

A company in Berkeley, Calif., has brought out "Gummy Lawyers," a chewy candy in the shape of a shark.

This latest insult to members of the bar is the brainchild of Nolo Press, Inc., a 19-year-old company specialized in legal self-help books and computer programs.

Each package of four blue shark-shaped candies comes with a booklet purporting to explain the species.

For example: Sharks "are equipped with fine senses of smell that allow them to detect minute dilutions of blood" up to a quarter-mile away. "Precisely the distance a hopeful personal-injury lawyer will run behind an ambulance to toss a business card," the booklet adds.

"We sort of had to do it," explained Barbara Kate Repa, a lawyer, who wrote the booklet, which costs $9.95 (with four candies). "Lawyers seemed to be getting more and more sanctimonious.

"The shark has become the national emblem of the profession."

The Arizona Reublic, Feb. 28, 1990

It was so cold in Prescott one day, I saw a lawyer with his hands in his own pockets.

The Author's Collection

⚖

An appeal, Hennessy, is when you ask one court to show its contempt for another court.

Finley Peter Dunne

⚖

What else is new?—a client had just been over-charged by his lawyer. The attorney attempted to mollify the angry client by citing a long list of famous people who were lawyers. Mahatma Ghandi, for example.

"Son of a gun," said the client. "The way he dressed, I'd have sworn he was a client."

The Author's Collection

⚖

The houses of lawyers are roofed with the skins of litigants.

Welsh proverb

⚖

After the rogues, what honest people dread most of all is a court of law.

A. Tournier

⚖

In law, nothing is certain but the expense.

Samuel Butler

⚖

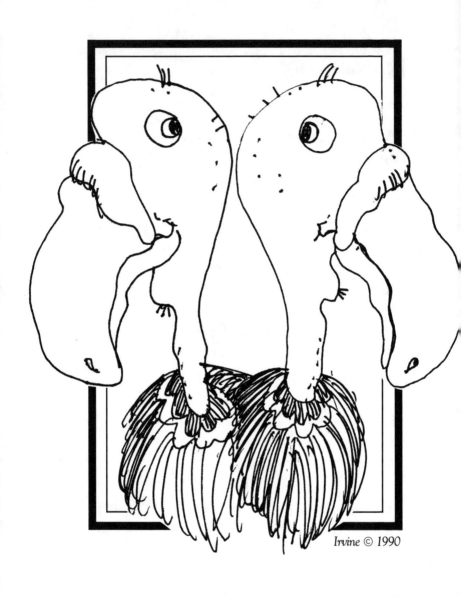

Irvine © 1990

What the difference between a lawyer and a
vulture? A lawyer qualifies for frequent flier credits.

Steiger's Ornithological Comparison.

⚖

A thousand starve, a few are fed,
Legions of robbers rack the poor,
The rich man steals the widow's bread,
And Lazarus dies at Dives' door;
The Lawyer and the Priest adjust
The claims of Luxury and Lust
To seize the earth and hold the soil,
To store the grain they never reap;
Under their heels the white slaves toil,
While children wail and women weep!

Robert Buchanan, 1841-1901, Scottish poet, novelist, playwright

⚖

Don't put no constrictions on da people. Leave 'em
ta hell alone.

Jimmy Durante, 1893-1980, American comedian

⚖

Put a lawyer on a spit, and you can always hire
another lawyer to turn it.

A Verity from The Author

⚖

Client, n. A Person who has made the customary
choice between the two methods of being robbed
legally.

Ambrose Bierce

⚖

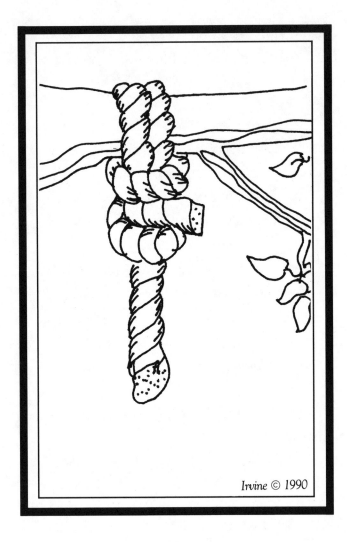

Irvine © 1990

How do you get a lawyer out of a tree?
Cut the rope.

Art Mehagian

Here is a quote from New York Governor Mario Cuomo: "Better to be a mouse in the jaws of a cat, than to be a citizen in the hands of a lawyer."

The Author's Collection

⚖

While lawyers keep careful accounts of their own time, and are not above stiffing clients by the quarter hour, in their own dealings they can be cheaper than swap meet socks. One lawyer's intern was overheard to say, "He pays me $30,000 a year. Fifty bucks a week in cash, and the rest in legal advice."

It is alleged.

⚖

Lawyer: "When I was a child, I yearned to become a pirate."

Client: "Congratulations."

⚖

The law doth punish man or woman
That steals the goose from the common,
But lets the greater felon loose,
That steals the common from the goose.

Anonymous, New England ditty, 1764

⚖

What is a lawyer? A man who gets two men to strip for a fight, then steals their clothes.

The Author's Collection

⚖

Sam the Beginning Horseman

IV. Don on Sam
A Minimal Apology

Germane to the thesis postulated by Sam Steiger in this smallish book was a cartoon appearing prominently on a page of the mainly straightforward *Wall Street Journal*, as the last weeks of the 1980s slipped away.

On the lap of Santa Claus perched a small child who had just been asked the customary question: "And have you been a good little boy?"

The lad replied: "I decline to answer on advice of my counsel."

Undeniably, America has become a litigious nation, populated by perhaps the most insidiously disputive people on an inherently quarrelsome planet. Or in the observation of former Arizona governor Jack Williams, "The world will end with neither a bang nor a whimper. The world will end in litigation." An otherwise benevolent sage, Jack Smith of the *Los Angeles Times*, periodically hauls the legal system to the dock for examination under typical headlines, "The Home of the Brave Is Becoming the Land of the Lawsuit." Jack finds it absurd that, "...tort lawyers hold that somebody is responsible for every accident, and it is not the victim. God, fate and luck has nothing to do with it."

Whether there are, indeed, too many lawyers as Sam Steiger maintains, or there are still not enough (as many lawyers contend), the man who would reduce their numbers, at age 61 has reached the old age of youth (or the youth of old age) with scarcely one dull day behind him.

Sam was born in New York City, the only child of Lewis and Reba K. Steiger, both now deceased. A moderately well-off family, they resided in a Manhattan apartment not far from Central Park. Lewis oversaw a prosperous wholesale garment business of national scale, while Reba doted upon her psychically happy, physically hale and mentally healthy son. Sam was given the advantage of private instruction at the Ethical Culture School in the Bronx ("That's when I did my homework...an hour each way on the subway.")

Although himself insulated from want, Sam through the 1930s prevailed over an impressionistic boyhood when the international trauma called the Great Depression was absorbed along with mother's lullabies and father's table talk. Each morning's *New York Times* told of more misery. Saturday newsreels flickered widespread privation: 25 percent national unemployment; Hoovervilles of the homeless subsisting on jackrabbit stew and stale bread; ragtag protesters skirmishing in Washington's parks; strong, proud men peddling apples and pencils on streetcorners; and widespread hunger and illness. The Steigers never missed a meal, yet along with millions of other survivors, they learned the worth of having something put by for a rainy day besides a freshly washed car.

Too young to serve in World War II, Sam vicariously flew a Hurricane in the Battle of Britain, routed Rommel out of Africa, hit Omaha Beach in the first wave, helped Ira Hayes raise Old Glory at Iwo and fingered the line for Admiral Tojo to sign in surrender on the fantail of the *U.S.S. Missouri*.

Destiny designed a discreet value system for many American males born in 1929. This I know, because I was born also on the Eastern Seaboard just six days after Sam. Our formative years were shaped by images of wrenching, large-scale happenings in which we became intimately involved in their smaller parts. At age 8 Sam was cleaning livery stables in Central Park for pocket change. I, delivering *The Washington Post*. In the 1930s the American work ethic opened an enterprise for every family member, however young. "No work, no eat," was my own immigrant Dad's 24-hour solution to national welfare expansion. No doubt Lewis Steiger would have nodded approval.

After Pearl Harbor the children of America staffed the scrap drives, tilled the Victory Gardens and sculpted silhouette models of enemy aircraft to aid allied ack-ack gunners in identification schools. From age 12 to 17 boys born in 1929 progressively assumed their blood would stain the shores of Imperial Japan during the final assault. Then abruptly, reprieve came as a product of yet another cataclysmic occurrence, the dropping of the Atom Bomb.

Sam graduated from the private Fieldston School and briefly bowed to his parents' choice of Cornell University. But the fondness for horses acquired at the stables drew Sam westward, to Colorado A&M (now Colorado State University) at Fort Collins. In 1950 he earned a bachelor of science degree in animal production. He drifted down to Northeastern Arizona to work as a cowboy for Bill Spence on the Steeple X Ranch near Springerville, in Northeastern Arizona. In 1950 that is where Uncle Sam delivered Korea War draft greetings to Nephew Sam.

Basic. Officer candidate school. Tank training. Korea duty. In the manner of most men tempered in the crucible of combat, Sam Steiger many years later only reluctantly shares his memories. But in response to a friend's wish for historical accuracy, the man broke a long silence with the following:

> My company commander to my knowledge had never been very far forward. Yet he ordered himself rearward to divisional headquarters for the purpose of receiving a medal for valor.
>
> This left me in charge of the company, heavily engaged with the Red Chinese Army. One night a kid staggered into my command post to report that the enemy had cut off one of our battalion's tanks. It was only a matter of time before the Chinese would burn it or blow it up.
>
> Since nobody else seemed eager to go, I took it upon myself to crawl for about two hours through enemy lines to our tank. I wriggled underneath and pounded on the escape hatch. The soldiers inside at first were leery, then one of them opened the

hatch a crack and exclaimed, "Hey, it's the
kike from Able Company!"

The men followed me, again crawling
a couple of hours to our own lines. On the
way we drew enemy mortar fire, and a
piece of shrapnel stuck me in the arm.
Not much of a hit.

For the deed First Lieutenant Steiger was awarded
the Purple Heart and the Silver Star, America's third-
highest military decoration for gallantry in action.

With the war suspended unwon, Sam was
honorable discharged in 1953. By the following year he
assumed a title and residency which he unwaveringly
has listed ever since: rancher, Prescott, Arizona. At an
altitude of one mile above sea level in the midst of a
vast ponderosa pine forest, Arizona's old territorial
capital ever has been something of a closed-circuit,
cultural cul-de-sac. Off the main east-west highways
and of late deprived of its dead-end railroad, Prescott
passed through the middle of the twentieth century
intact: a community with a central, shaded courthouse
square and a population almost entirely waspish and
sprinkled with fourth-generation Kirklands, Ruffners,
Heads, Gardners and Goldwaters.

Fifty years after statehood an imperial coalition of
ranching and mining interests had dominated Arizona
government. Prescott's city and surrounding Yavapai
County wielded political clout disproportionate to its
paucity of voters. Registered Democrats outnumbered
Republicans eight to one. Never a large town, Prescott

summers attracted the social elite of Phoenix, they seeking cool mountain respite from the sizzling desert. Before noon the next day, all of Prescott would know who slugged whom at the long, stand-up bar of the Palace Saloon on Whiskey Row. Or which livestock at what price were bought and sold with a handshake in the lobby of the Hassayampa or St. Michael's.

Could a Jewish Manhattanite in his mid-20s of Republican persuasion presume to swap ponies and gain friends among such a closed-circuit Christian colony tracing its roots to the Genesis of American Arizona government in 1864? That he did. He easily slipped into Levi's and lizard boots, bellied up at the Palace, converted his Big Apple accent into Western speech patterns, earned a reputation as a shrewd dealer in horseflesh, called the races at Prescott Downs, married into a Prescott first family and spoke his mind all over town.

The latter trait soon would become both his charm and curse. "Shooting from the lip," was Prescott's phrase for it. Sam was obliged to defend himself more than once in the presence of eventful cowpunchers. Some stuffier Prescott elements wrote Sam off as an Eastern blowhard, but the man's humor and candor were generally appreciated. When, in 1960, he entered politics, he took on a longtime Democrat encumbent, Charles X. (Chick) Orme, from a family as old as granite. Orme was so confident of victory he vacationed in Europe during the campaign. Sam clomped up on back porches and shot the bull wherever he smelled a vote. Then at the polls interloper Steiger ate patrician Orme like grapes.

Sam's next hurdle was Arizona's most exclusive club, the Ol' Boy, 28-member Arizona Senate. Almost from Day One the freshman senator took on the Democratic leadership including the Senate president. He delivered a Lincoln Day floor speech assailing tax exemptions for widows and veterans, "enough," as one reporter opined, "to send a 50,000-vote shudder through the entire legislative body."

Scarcely pausing for breath, Steiger demanded that the quasi-municipal Salt River (reclamation and power) Project begin to pay taxes. He rammed through a bill to that effect, and followed with legislation providing taxation on church property not connected with religious activities. Then in the closing days of the 1962 term, Steiger in the Senate broke with tradition to accuse six members of the House of taking bribes. Amid cries to censure the outspoken Steiger, Arizona's attorney general announced there was *indeed* sufficient information to prosecute the Representatives. But a county attorney refused to act. In the end, nobody went to jail, but five of the six failed to return to the Legislature.

Blackballed by many establishment politicians, Steiger with luck and panache endeared himself to his constituency. "Rarely favored, always win," Sam taunted his opponents, and sure enough, the next election he led the Yavapai legislative ticket. He had a knack for making news. Running for Congress in 1964 he converted a horse trailer into a speaking platform, named it *Major Hoopla*, and dragged it 30,000 miles from town to town. During that campaign, barnstorming by air around Arizona's farflung Third Congressional District, his light aircraft was forced down by carburetor icing in the remote, mountainous Apache Indian Reservation. After his rescue next day, Steiger was asked how he and his pilot kept warm through the chilly night.

Affecting an expression of intense pain, Sam croaked: "I...a politician...was subjected to the ultimate indignity. I had...to burn...my campaign literature!" *Vox populi.* In a district 3.2 Democratic to 1 Republican, Sam Steiger lost by only 800 votes. Undaunted, he signed on several newspapers and radio stations, and went to Vietnam as a war correspondent. Soon Steiger's eyewitness accounts of infantry life and death illustrated with better-than-average newsphotos were trickling back to his clients, readers and listeners. "Our Man Sam in 'Nam" slogged through paddies, sweated out guerrilla ambushes and chronicled the stories of American young men and women mired in a misunderstood and increasingly unpopular war.

When Steiger in 1966 ran again for Congress in a district of eight northern counties and part of another, parents and grandparents remembered who had trooped with their youngsters in the jungles and swamps. Steiger pointed to his own state senate voting record (missing only 2 percent of 1,365 roll call votes in four years) in contrast to the Congressional incumbent (179 missed votes, the worst individual record in the last session of the 89th Congress). This time, Steiger went to Washington.

Within three months the Congressional newcomer was quoted (he staunchly insists, misquoted) on news-wires that the Nation's Capitol sheltered more than its share of drunks, and "others so incompetent I wouldn't hire them to push a wheelbarrow." A furor similar to the state senate uproar gained Steiger national fame and relegation to Congress's woodshed.

Shrugging off the stigma, he introduced four pieces of legislation and got two passed, an above-average accomplishment for a freshman. Easily reelected, he maintained his high profile by muckraking dog and horse racing operators. For months, years, Steiger took on what he said was mob control of track management and wagering. Lawsuits, contempt proceeding and public relations assaults against him notwithstanding, in the end the president of one of Steiger's fattest racing targets publicly admitted ties to Mafia figures.

Many of Steiger's political leanings were vintage Republican. Law and order. Reduced government meddling and spending. Tough on expansionist Communism. Gun control won't work. Too much bureaucracy. Paperwork, suffocating the system. But a day scarcely passed that he didn't break loose a Social Security check for a qualified but confused constituent, or deliver a deed of land ownership to a band of Yavapai Apaches squatting near the white man's town of Payson. "That's all that really matters," Steiger told a reporter over a cafeteria breakfast in Washington in 1964. "Helping people."

In 1975 fate and folly delivered to the résumé of Sam Steiger an entry which undoubtedly will hound him to his last days. One late afternoon he learned that not far from his mountain ranch several burros were being held in a pen after being rounded up from a highway right-of-way. There had been hard feelings in the area over stray stock and alleged fence-cutting. Armed with a borrowed rifle Steiger went to the pens, he said, to inspect brands and establish ownership. The donkeys, enraged by neglect and abuse, charged him, heels kicking. He killed two. The man has been mercilessly ragged by friend and foe every since.

Having served five terms in Congress, in a manner so affrontive to liberals that Ralph Nader issued a 30,000-word white paper exposing Steiger's consistent conservatism, Sam raised his sights to the U.S. Senate. There followed a bitterly mean-spirited and mutually destructive brawl in the Republican primary with fellow Congressman John Conlan, fiesty son of Big League Umpire Jocko Conlan. The contest eventually spilled ink onto the front page of the *Wall Street Journal*, which called it "a rancid exercise in democracy," and "the year's meanest Senate campaign." Steiger won the primary, but not without cost. The reputations of both men were tattered. Some analysts for the first time in Sam's political career adjudged his subsequent general election campaign as "arrogant and ineffective." He lost to Democrat Dennis DeConcini.

"And there are those who wish not to believe this," claims Sam, "but I am one of very few to spend ten years in Washington, and come home poorer than when I went."

The next five or six years brought mixed fortune. His two marriages had come apart. His saving grace, humor, often abandoned him, to be replaced with unbecoming sarcasm. Picayunish civil disputes arose from some of his business dealings. Ink spilled when Sam insulted the highway patrolman who issued two speeding tickets in the same stretch of road in three days. Given space to write a local newspaper column, Sam explored the frontiers of libel. He resorted to name-calling in environmental debates (and to be fair, so did others). When he appeared in what now had become his costume—runover boots, sagging denims, broad crimson suspenders, unlighted pipe or cigar clamped in his teeth—at Prescott City Council meetings, citizens and council members squirmed. He was accused of selling out to copper interests and other developers. Understandably so—in that Sam by his nature gravitated to the causes of economic development and free enterprise. In those days even Sam growled at a reporter, "You have to line up to hate Steiger these days."

By 1982 he had changed his registration to Libertarian, he said, tongue in cheek, "to get off Republican fund-raising mailing lists," and had agreed to run for governor. The real reason: Libertarians were weary of circulating petitions to qualify for places on the ballot.

If they could deliver five percent of the vote in the general election, permanent ballot status for the Libertarian Party would be gained. Thus, "the deal with the Devil," as a Libertarian leader was overheard to say.

Nobody took Steiger's candidacy seriously, least of all himself.

Asked if he could win: "Oh, my God, no! Come on, be reasonable!"

The love-hate relationship that Steiger enjoyed-endured with *The Arizona Republic* turned treacle, as in one lead editorial: "Just as it seemed that Arizona might suffer through another gray gubernatorial campaign consumed with serious issues, high country rancher Sam Steiger has come riding to the rescue.... Steiger's reputation as a witty and brawling public figure...casts an unfair shadow over his service in Congress, which many observers in retrospect believe was exemplary." The editorial concluded, "Despite Steiger's inability to become governor, his entry into the race has the welcome quality of adding wit and color to an otherwise tedious affair."

The ploy worked. Satan Sam tempted five percent of Arizona to vote Libertarian. And to a degree, perhaps, Sam transported himself to a higher level of personal liberty. He would not be the first or last politician to be hypnotized by his own voice. The tendency manifested itself in May, 1986 in Prescott's Great Crosswalk Caper. Sam's role in the affair would make him whole again—at least in the eyes of most of his home townspeople.

For at least fifty years a painted line walk had

served the courthouse lunch crowd and evening barhoppers wishing to cross Montezuma Street (Whiskey Row) at midblock. But during a Spring repaving the State Department of Transportation obliterated and refused to repaint the walk. In fact, the walk was blocked by stripes designating curbside parking spaces. As their excuse, highway authorities expressed silly concerns for pedestrian safety and public liability.

The word from on high: "There will be no goddam crosswalk." For months Prescott seethed with resentment. This was, after all, the street to which the foundling town had removed itself from Granite Creek, "because the sight of water made the customers sick." On Whiskey row an early restaurant offered: "Breakfast, fried venison and chili. Dinner, roast venison and chili, or chili and beans. Supper, chili." Not far outside this town in those times a woman dispatched a note from her fortress cabin to her husband shopping in town: "Dear Lewis, I'm about out of ammunition. Please send more."

In 1873 the Prescott *Miner* published a list of four hundred persons slain by Indians. This was the neighborhood where, in 1889, legend says Prescott lost the territorial capital by one vote when a Prescott supporter failed to answer roll call, explaining later that a lady of the evening had swallowed his glass eye. Montezuma was the street where cowboy Frank Condron rode a bull buffalo for $1,000 in gold. Not even the disastrous conflagration of 1900 shut down

Whiskey Row—the patrons simply picked up the back bars and set them down across the street, with business resuming as usual. For years this was the setting of a certain high class service business behind a carved oak door whose etched-glass motto read, "Caveat Emptor."

As Marguerite Noble relates, Prescott was where:

> *Dick Robbins, old time rodeo hand, was holed up in a hotel room with some of his fellow contestants. The boys were celebrating with liquid refreshments.... This particular evening, one ol' boy, quite likkered up, declared he could jump out of the window and fly around the building. The bets were on. The performer staggered to an open window, waved his arms toward the heavens—and jumped. The landing in the bushes below sobered him. Wobbling dazed back into the room, he attacked his partner's loyalty with, "Why'd you let me do that?" His partner hiccuped and explained, "I thought you could do it. I lost ten dollars on you."*

Irvine © 1990

And now, some officious martinet in the highway department down at Phoenix was intimating that those hick stumblebums up at Prescott couldn't be trusted to walk across their own street.

One Friday night, with sixty onlookers cheering, Steiger emerged from the Palace. By now Sam's once-svelte physique was amply padded. Beer and raw beef had added to his girth, and years of riding (or strutting) had imparted a bow in the legs. An old straw hat was mashed down to his ears. Cigar aglow, he laid down double lines of yellow, traffic-resistant street paint from sidewalk to sidewalk. By the time police arrived, Steiger, assisted by allies, had completed diagonal lines—a bit wavy perhaps, but functional. The cops wrote him a ticket for criminal damage.

In the ensuing trial in Justice Court before a jury, the prosecution asserted that Steiger's al fresco artwork was inept and dangerous. Crews were obliged to cover the yellow paint with gray—thus a cost inferring criminal damage. Steiger as his own counsel retorted that he was merely restoring a historical feature more than a half-century old. He said the crosswalk embodied the spirit of Prescott. And who owned the streets, anyway? The people!

The jury deliberated twenty minutes and aquitted the man. The effect on him was the pouring of the gasoline of free thought upon a bonfire of rebellion. Sam, as his old ironic self, filled time on a local daily radio talk show, and space in a Prescott weekly to express his contrarian, often outrageous opinions.

It was on June 11, 1987 that he wrote most strongly of lawyers: "Shun lawyers, ignore lawyers, but above all, do not elect them to public office.... Lawyers are the running sores of the twentieth century, and if they are not isolated and done away with as humanely as instinct will permit, they will be the cause of the downfall of this culture."

Steiger put forth a plan for ending the federal deficit. "Set a salary of $150,000 for each member of Congress. Then take away $10,000 in salary for each billion dollars the budget is over the limit. It would take a few years, but you'd have a balanced budget. The problem of politicians is they all have self-interests. Hell, that's the nature of humankind. But with my plan, some of that self-interest would go out the window."

The election of Evan Mecham to the office of Governor—his besieged, truncated term of office—and Arizona's agony through the first impeachment and conviction of an American governor since 1929 is a much larger story in itself. But as the underdog Mecham soundly trounced two primary opponents and prevailed over the Democratic woman candidate, Steiger was entrained in his most powerful yet perilous adventure in public life. He was hired by the new governor as a top aide to oversee, among other agencies, the State Department of Transportation.

Within days a full crew of state highway workers appeared at Whiskey Row. They neatly, professionally, permanently painted a magnificent yellow, curb-to-curb crosswalk at midblock.

When asked for an explanation, the governor's brand-new assistant replied innocently, "A coincidence."

But at large lurched forces too powerful to shunt aside with clever moves and quick quips. Mecham had refused to kowtow to preelection editorial boards; sought not the support of the state's dominant newspapers. Publicly spurned, establishment media publishers, editors and producers made little attempt to disguise their loathing of the gadfly car dealer who for a quarter century in his own newspapers and broadsides had opposed, embarrassed and belittled their political kingmaking and governmental manipulating within Arizona's power structure. Certain reporters sensing careers to be made or lost, pounced upon Mecham in a journalistic feeding frenzy unprecedented since territorial times. And Mecham, fervent true believer and feckless speaker, obliged the omnipresent press with gaffe after gaffe.

In time, Arizona would contemplate three courses for removing Mecham from office. He was subject to a recall election, and the attorney general filed criminal charges alleging misuse of campaign monies. Those citizens who believed the first two of these processes should be fully resolved, were flattened by the media steamroller for impeachment. Both the House and Senate meekly obliged. Mecham was impeached in the House, tried and found guilty of "high crimes and misdemeanors" in the Senate and removed from office. After the fact, a jury found Mecham innocent, "vilified by his enemies, vindicated by his peers," as a newsman wrote. The people of Arizona will never know how their recall election would have turned out. Authorities arbitrarily cancelled the election.

It was during the 1987 year of feverish press scrutiny, that Sam Steiger did something stunningly stupid. By telephone he ordered a state parole board member to vote for the governor's choice of executive secretary. Sam told the man if he did not do the governor's bidding, the man would probably lose his part time job as justice of the peace.

Shortly after that conversation was completed, the board member called Sam back. Sam went through the whole thing again. This time, there was a difference. Agents of the attorney general's office tape recorded what they thought was damning evidence. It was, needless to say, the way that government had been run in Arizona—nay, the entire nation—since the governor of the Massachusets Bay Colony told his harbormaster to fish or cut bait. Straining the language of the statute far beyond its limits, Attorney General Robert Corbin brought charges against Sam Steiger of extortion, a felony punishable by a fine of $150,000 and three to five years in the prison system that Steiger had been bossing for nine months. Under the hot glare of the press, Steiger in November, 1987 resigned from his post as aide to the governor.

"You're damn right I'm scared," the man confided to a friend at the time. "The attorney general whom I repeatedly have accused of building a dynasty of the largest number of lawyers per capita in the United States now is certain he has me right where he wants me."

Not quite. A mob braved a nippy outdoor night to raise defense funds at a barbecue dinner and auction at Rawhide, the Western amusement park north of Scottsdale. Attending were many of Arizona's shakers and doers. At this gathering, at least, the prevailing sentiment was that Sam had been enticed by a disloyal appointee, and entrapped by vindictive government lawyers. Steiger's case was taken by Tom Karas, a lawyer of such skill and style, he later would become president of the state bar.

At the trial, the prosecution contended that something of material value—a part time job—was put at risk in a conversation between Steiger, the governor's functionary, and the parole board member, the governor's appointee. This amounted to extortion.

In effect, the defense countered that this was not an extortion of a material value, but merely the way that political cows have devoured political cabbages in America forever. If a governor could not influence his board member to vote in favor of the governor's preference for filling a related position, all other things considered equal, how could this be construed as extortion?

The jury found Sam guilty. Before sentence was passed, 170 letters from afar and from Arizona's thought leaders, landed in the chambers of Judge Ronald Reinstein, who proclaimed from the bench, "Lo and behold, even from a few lawyers."

Before him loomed a large and prideful man, chin up, unrepentant, at the judge's mercy.

Anything to say? The convict expressed no remorse. Instead, he once again verbally skinned the attorney general alive.

Judge Reinstein heard him out, then averred, "I really don't think jail would in any way change your mind about accepting responsibility for the case."

Steiger nodded. "I do not believe I am retrainable." The judge stiffed Sam with four years probation and fined him $4,500, which some citizens thought lenient and some did not, considering that the man had never previously committed a crime, and who had done a universe of good for his constituents. Some of Sam Steiger's supporters questioned the propriety of yet another condition of the sentence: 700 hours of menial clerking, to be performed for the Bar of Arizona. In affixing this requirement to the reformation of Sam Steiger, Judge Reinstein openly expressed great pleasure.

By the self-satisfied relish of Judge Reinstein, one was reminded of a timeless limerick:

> There was an old justice named Percival,
> Who said, "I suppose you'll get worse if I'll
> Send you to jail,
> So I'll put you on bail."
> Now wasn't Judge Percival merciful?

The smirk must have turned to shock when all this tedium was thrown out in a unanimous ruling by the State Court of Appeals. The opinion found the statute unconstitutionally vague and jeopardizing of free speech. Further, "it provides insufficient guidance to those who must make demands on others, and because it permits arbitrary and discriminatory enforcement." Incredibly, the attorney general toyed with an urge to challenge this appellate rebuff all the way to the Arizona Supreme Court, adding more tens of thousands of taxpayer dollars to the mounting costs of his failed prosecutions. Steiger thereby was kept twisting on the edges of his nerves for another, unneccessary sixty days before Attorney General Corbin capitulated. By this time, too, the Democratic governor who succeeded Republican Mecham had outright fired the parole board member who allegedly was extorted by Sam. Wonderful.*

Through it all, for the best part of a year, Steiger had worn the label of convicted felon—and all the humility and loss of citizenship which that status proscribes—with unflagging humor, dauntless courage and profane rebellion. To their credit, Sam's two grown sons and daughter quietly rallied to his side. This social participant was afforded the opportunity which is denied many of life's critical spectators: to come to know who are one's true friends. And the friends who stuck by him, the meaning of Norman Douglas's maxim, "To find a friend, you must close one eye— to keep him, two."

* As this book is printed, this firing also is on appeal.

That Sam Steiger, of all the rascals holding
Arizona state office during the mid-1980s, in and
out of the Mecham administration, should be the
one to do hard time, struck some of us as a gross
miscarriage. Aromas of revenge, framing, duplicity,
coercion and overreaching ambition polluted
Arizona's political atmosphere in those years, and
their stenches linger still.

For weeks the people of Arizona were provided
the rare opportunity to eyewitness, live, the perfor-
mance in chambers of their representatives. Not all
of them by any means, but enough to give a populace
pause, unintentionally unmasked themselves as tongue-
tied orators, pompous asses, special interest lackeys and
inept thinkers. Dissuaded by public outcries from its
initial lust to hold the impeachment proceedings in
secret, the Legislature was obliged to put itself on
public display. The result was not the Legislature's finest
hour. To the contrary, the prevailing denominator was
so appallingly low, few figures survived intact and ennobled,
as did Francis X. Gordon, upon whom as Chief Justice of
the Arizona Supreme Court, the constitution thrust the
duty of impeachment Presiding Officer.

There was, in retrospect, only one sublime, elegant
moment in the protracted Mecham indictment and
trial, aired gavel to gavel over public television,
examined in millions of words of print and diagnosed
in thousands of hours of radio broadcasts.

Sam Steiger, a piece of work wearing ranch boots, a
western cut suit and suspenders and an air of supreme

confidence, was on the stand before Mecham's jury, Arizona's senators.

Another rare quality act, special prosecutor Paul Eckstein, intellectually circled Sam with the well advised wariness of a white hunter approaching a wounded bull elephant in tall grass.

Eckstein closely questioned Steiger on conversations Steiger had had with the governor since resigning his post as aide. Sam was being, well, creatively dissimulative, for Eckstein could be disarmingly deft in drawing damaging testimony from a defense witness. A bit exasperated, Eckstein:

> Q. *Mr. Steiger, you believe that it's important to put quotations in context, don't you.*
> A. *Yes, sir.*
>
> Q. *You talked about that sign you had on your door, "the first thing we do is kill all the lawyers."*
> A. *Yes, sir.*
>
> Q. *Comes from a Shakespeare play.*
> A. *Yes, sir.*
>
> Q. *Do you know which play it comes from.*
> A. *Henry the VI.*
>
> Q. *Do you know what immediately precedes that?*
> A. *No, and if it's going to mitigate the contents, I don't want to know, counsel.*
>
> Q. *Mr. Steiger, I would like you to know, and I'm not enough of a Shakespearean scholar*

to quote it exactly, but it goes something like this: "If we want justice and corruption to run rampant over the land, the first thing we do is kill all the lawyers."

A. Oh, Counselor, I think that is a legal construction of what otherwise is a very cogent phrase.

Q. I gather you didn't have the entire phrase.

A. No, I did not, sir.

Q. I gather in your distaste and dislike for lawyers, Attorney General Corbin stood at the top of that list and stands at the top of that list today.

A. Is that a question.

Q. Yes.

A. I think that's an unfair characterization. My concern about Attorney General Corbin has almost nothing to do with his being a lawyer, because I've never been convinced that he has played that role, and my concern about him is based upon the political role that he plays.

That was not news. News was, Eckstein's apparent brilliant literary scholarship threatened to parry Steiger's favorite, lifelong thrust. In fact, the direction of the blade was reversed. For if Eckstein had the gist of the passage correct, Shakespeare's character was cautioning *against* the doing away with lawyers, who stood between civilization and barbaritry.

That night, that segment of Arizona which cares about such niceties, consulted *Bartlett's* and the *Collected Works*. For if Eckstein could deprive Steiger his battlecry from the Bard, poor Sam would not have much left.

Yet when Sam Steiger returned to the stand it was with some of the brimming bounce of his days as a college football player. Now he was under the friendly examination of a defense attorney, Jerris Leonard.

> *Q. Did there come a point in time when you learned about the $80,000 loan [of the Governor's Protocol Fund] to Mecham Pontiac.*
>
> *A. Yes, sir.*
>
> *Q. Did you formulate an opinion as to whether that was an appropriate investment of the money.*
>
> *A. Yes, sir.*
>
> *Q. What was that opinion.*
>
> *A. I thought it was stupid politically, but I at no time considered that it was illegal.*
>
> *Q. Why was that.*
>
> *A. Very simply because I knew of no statute that dictated how the money would be held until it was spent. And my understanding was that this was a loan that was to be repaid at a time certain, and therefore, it was not in violation of any statute,*

because I knew of no statute, and know of no statute today, that dictates the manner in which the money will be held until it is spent.

Q. Do you recall during your previous testimony that Mr. Eckstein had some colloquy about a quote from Shakespeare.

A. Yes, sir.

Q. Have you since that time done some research on that subject.

A. Yes, sir.

Q. And what has that research developed.

A. I was hoping you would ask that question, sir.

THE PRESIDING OFFICER (Chief Justice Gordon): I wish you would, because I looked it up, too, counselor.

THE WITNESS: I thank the Presiding Officer. The quote is from Part Two, Act IV, Scene II of a Shakespeare effort known as Henry the VI. I took the trouble to copy the page on which the statement appears. I'll share with you the preceding statement, which if you will recall counsel [Eckstein] described to me as saying, and I am paraphrasing, and I couldn't hope to achieve the eloquence of counsel, but he said something about if you would have raping and pillage in the land, you would first kill all the lawyers.

I quote, I do not interpret, I quote:

"Cade...."—Cade, I believe—and I must confess to you, all I have read of *Henry the VI* is this page.

THE PRESIDING OFFICER: Are we going to hear **the whole** (emphasis provided) page?

THE WITNESS: No, no. I understand the urgency, Mr. Presiding Officer.

Cade is the gentleman who I believe is going to become Henry the VI. He said:
"Cade. I thank you, good people: there shall be no money; all shall eat and drink on my score; and I will apparel them all in one livery, that they may agree like brothers, and worship me their lord."

[Then I quote Dick] a character known as the Butcher, which I find effective: "The first thing we do, let's kill all the lawyers."

The following speech—and I really particularly love this, and I hope you will share my enthusiasm:

"Cade. Nay, that I mean to do."

Which implies that he was already going to do that, kill all the lawyers.

"Is this not a lamentable thing, that of the skin of an innocent lamb should be made parchment! that parchment, being scribbled o'er, should undo a man?"

*In other words, why kill a lamb to make a
piece of parchment to make a man a lawyer?
Now, I submit to you, there is nothing in there
that redeems the virtue of the profession. And,
counselor [Leonard], I know it was a great
personal sacrifice that you let me do that, but
I thank you. And I did want to set the record
straight.*

*And I firmly believe that counsel for the
House Managers [Eckstein] believed that
nobody could have ever written something like
that, because I think they teach that to lawyers
in law school, that that is really not intended
to be what I am telling you here, that at least
William Shakespeare meant it for real.*

With that, the defense offered Steiger either for
cross-examination or cross-testimony.

"It was the single class act of the entire hearings,"
commented Phoenix *New Times* columnist Tom
Fitzpatrick, "and it was memorable because Steiger was
not only smarter than his questioners, but funnier as well,"

Smarter than Paul Eckstein? I doubt that. Funnier,
yes. Eckstein, having met his better in the world of
theater if not the courtroom, would have no more of
Shakespeare's Plays 101, as interpreted by the livestock
husbandryman from Prescott. The testimony thereafter
droned on regarding who knew what and when about
the Protocol Fund. Except for an occasional, cautionary
complaint from an isolated, learned Senator, or bleat by

an Elizabethan England scholar, Steiger was left with his major premise intact.

Kill the lawyers. Shakespeare said it, and meant it.

Even before the Court of Appeals overturned Steiger's conviction—it had to be a bone in the throat for Superior Court Judge Ronald Reinstein, who embraced the daft idea that bossing a public hireling could be construed as extortion—Sam went public as a television, radio and print commentator. Thus far in America, anyway, a convicted felon continued to possess the right to free speech. And whereas in Arizona a felon cannot vote or hold office or pack a firearm, the license of expression remains. Here are some of the public utterances from a man of three decades in state and national politics. Those who know Sam well equate his words with 100-proof sour mash bourbon, distilled for effect, but probably best swallowed with a splash of branch water provided by the consumer. I have considerably edited these paragraphs for length, but Sam got final review:—

- *Steiger's Law: "Whenever you create a structure with a public mission...the structure always becomes more important than the mission.*

- *On his singular accomplishment in politics: "In Congress in 1972 by force of will on the floor of the House, I killed a Land Use Planning bill that permanently would have required federal approval of every development right down to a single family dwelling in the entire United States. That bill very nearly* passed, and it would have, had I not killed it. It would have been the lifetime guaranteed employment act for lawyers."

- Advice to bar associations: "A protective syndrome of some bar associations for their members is one cause of weakening of public faith in the legal profession and the American system of jurisprudence. And it is not just the legal profession. All sorts of professional and trade groups do this. But it seems worse regarding law. Complicated statutes are written to protect the innocent-accused. Rogue lawyers twist these laws to protect the guilty-accused. The solution is for the various bar associations to look at themselves and change their code of ethics. In other words, control the avarice of that small percentage of members who twist the law for their own gain."

- Summing up regarding the Attorney General's suits: "They bombed on Mecham's trial, when a jury acquitted him of all charges. They failed in attempts to indict others. I was the only victory they had. The general perception was that I was a target because I worked for Mecham. That's just not true. The AG's office has turned into a tremendously overpriced empire. The real reason I was charged was because I was critical of the AG. And that's the kind of abusive power that can't be tolerated anywhere. Mine was a question of style. Theirs is a question of intent, and there's a hell of a difference."

• The perfection of the managed, packaged candidate: "If it wasn't so pervasively effective, it would be a joke. Professional campaign managers do their best to obscure the reality of candidates. The goal is to blur the image enough so voters won't know what they are getting, and to slur the opponent. Techniques of marketing instead of stands on issues now dominate campaigns. Seldom does it backfire. I'm fond of the story about a Rockefeller who went to the South to run for a national office and his professional manager produced television ads showing Rockefeller with his sleeves rolled up and leading a team of mules. His Republic opponent, Vinegar Bend Mizell, went on television with his own ads to urge voters to watch the Rockefeller ad, 'and to pay particular attention to the embarrassed expressions on the faces of the mules.' Rockefeller pulled the ads pronto. I'd put professional campaign managers out of business. They are a threat to democracy that I'm sure our founders did not anticipate. Good candidates should consider going public with this sort of statement: 'My opponent is being packaged and sold like bath soap, and I deplore this, and I'm not going to do it, and I think one of the reasons you should vote for me is

*that professional managers are making my
opponent into something he is not, something
that is salable, and I think that's disgusting.' "*

- *About privatization of governmental functions:
"I have always believed that virtually every
effort of government is a flawed effort. Now,
privatization is not magic, but I think it will be
superior, overall, to government effort because
the profit motive, while it offends many people,
puts some responsibility on the operator which
the government doesn't have. Given any
scenario, be it electricity, highways, prisons,
schools, any scenario that involves the private
sector more than it's involved now, will result
in a better product than we have now."*

The reader should understand that I do not agree
with all of compadre Steiger's opinions. Nor can I
totally embrace his exaggerated passion for a society
prospering sans lawyers. Perhaps the more important
book I've written examines the history of an Arizona
territorial range feud which erupted in a region devoid
of legal recourse, cost some fifty lives over a span of
fifteen years, and helped to hold back statehood before
law could be established.

Today we expect our lawyers to absorb much of our
emotional strain in times of crisis: divorce, estate
settlement, contract. The wicked ways of Washington
are largely blamed (fairly or unfairly) on lawyers. In
court, one-half of the lawyers lose, and losing clients
never forget or forgive. Experts say that the public wants

to believe that America's 800,000 lawyers earn much more than the $68,900 median pay reported by the American Bar Association.

Citing a statistic of 40,000 lawyers leaving the profession every year...about the same number entering law school...in the last month of the 1980s *Time* magazine asked rhetorically, "Why the mass dissatisfaction? A major increase in working hours, coupled with a corresponding rise in stress, has led to an erosion in the quality of life for many lawyers. Law firms often require that each year attorneys do 2,000 to 2,500 hours of work that can be billed to clients, almost a third more than a decade ago. That frequently translates into twelve-hour-plus workdays and busy weekends as well." Meantime, abetting in the public mind the image of moneyed, glamorous, luxurious lifestyle are television stereotypes such as *L.A. Law*. Thus, the law is perceived as the crabgrass in the lawn of life.

To the contrary, lawyers may deserve generously of our sympathy as well as ridicule. This minor barbed book is but one of a swarm of stinging productions and publications currently besetting lawyers. Danny DeVito's character in the dark comedy, *The War of the Roses*, asks, "What do you call 500 lawyers at the bottom of the ocean?" Answer: "A good start." In *Back to the Future Part II* the world is a far better place; lawyers have been outlawed.

Upon such evidence *USA Today* concludes, "Now it seems barrister bashing is the trendy sport for cynics in—and out—of the cinema." In the off-broadway hit,

Other People's Money, an actor playing a character with numerous lawyers avers, "They're like nuclear warheads. They have theirs so you need yours. But once you use them, they (muck) everything up." *Gentlemen's Quarterly* observes that "Lawyers and painters can soon change black to white." And author Peter Mayle tells how "...the most basic is the language problem. For their own obvious ends, lawyers have perfected an exclusive form of communication. It has a passing resemblance to English mixed with a smattering of dog Latin, but to the man in the street, it might just as well be Greek. Thus, when he receives a writ or a subpoena or one of the other countless arrows in the legal quiver, he is completely mystified. What does it mean? What can he do? What else but hire an interpreter—who is, of course, a lawyer. And there we have the kind of situation that lawyers love: The two sides can settle down to a protracted exchange of mumbo jumbo, most of it completely unintelligible to their clients and all of it charged at an hourly rate that defies belief."

The Washington Monthly predicts "anthropologists of the next generation will look back in amazement... the most ambitious and brightest were siphoned off the productive work force and trained to think like a lawyer." Recent books aimed at and even thrown at lawyers include the humorous *Skid Marks* (see Steiger's joke, page 8) and *What to do with a Dead Lawyer*, and the serious *Full Disclosure: Do you Really Want to Be a Lawyer?* and *Running from the Law: Why Good Lawyers Are Getting Out of the Profession.*

That said, I side foursquare with Sam's derision of the language of modern law. Lawyers—the original sin committed by law professors, more so than engineers or bankers or journalists (even)—mutilate our lyrical, lucid, logical Mother Tongue into a quackish, opaque, circumventing jargon. Bad enough that it is written and spoken within the legal system, the gawky language insidiously oozes out of the courtroom into the people's English. By the end of the House impeachment and Senate trial of otherwise inarticulate Governor Mecham, he, and half the Legislature and most press people were parroting the argot of the law.

My hero is Wisconsin Supreme Court Justice William A. Bablitch, whose eyes glazed over when a lawyer before him declared:

> The state's argument is the same as the argument of the court. That is to say, that is what the court did, and that is what the court does, then the court does what the court does, and if that is what the court does, it is all right....

In that moment Judge Bablitch began a six-year crusade to exorcize such maunders from law intercourse. In a recent article in *America West Airlines* magazine, fellow writer Brian Hickey quoted Justice Bablitch, "Lawyers have got some of the worst writing teachers of all—former judges using their own written opinions." And another bugaboo is the use of secret language to exclude non-lawyers: "Law students need to be told that legalese is not the key to the kingdom, communication is."

Eagerly awaited is the forthcoming latest tome by David Mellinkoff, law professor emeritus at the University of California at Los Angeles. Mellinkoff's *Dictionary of American Legal Usage* will contain such coinages:

> Lawsick., n., a peculiarly English-like language commonly used in writing about law; peculiar in the habitual indifference to ordinary usage of English words, grammar and punctuation; and in preferring the archaic, wordy, pompous and confusing over the clear, brief and simple; persists chiefly through a belief of its writers that these peculiarities lead to precision.

While joining in brother Steiger's alarm regarding America the Contentious and the costly legal profession the nation supports, I, as a 40-year journalist, lament as much or more the presumption, the hubris and the elitism which have become so pervasive in my own craft.

Consider only this day's all-but-complete sacrifice of personal privacy in the name of public interest. Time was, reporters accompanying a Harry S Truman campaign train, at the end of a newsday, might put away their notepads and engage the candidate in an earthy, convivial session of poker. The public may have had the right to know what it *needed* to know, but the press drew a line—fuzzy and elastic, perhaps—on revealing every detail possible vis a vis the private lives of public figures.

A generation later, largely at the instigation of the press, candidates meekly supply financial statements, submit to ruthless scrutiny of their life histories, and confess all youthful indescretions in the dock of the media's modern, extralegal tribunal. And woe be the aspiring public servant who ever held lust in his heart, smoked a joint, or cheated on a college exam. A man on heroic impulse might save the life of President Ford, and within hours have it known all over the world that he is gay.

"There are days when my wife wishes she would find my face in the refrigerator on the back of a milk carton," was the richly witty utterance of a candidate in the last Democratic presidential primary. But by the time the press blew up the one-liner into a federal case of insensitivity toward runaway kids, the man was obliged to hold a nationally broadcast press conference to express his remorse, regret and sorrow. Then paradoxically, the press in editorials takes the lead in wondering why better men and women do not seek public office.

Nor is the incessant, unrestrained, shameless prying limited to officials. With the press setting the example, revelation of the most intimate information has become the required American way. Want to open a checking account? Show your driver's license. Apply for a home loan? Hand over your income tax return. Seek a job? Produce a urine sample. All of which assists the enforcers, but savages the venerable American ethic of privacy.

Then one last comment. Nothing of human causation is forever. Lasting impressions are as scarce as the blizzards of Phoenix. Yet as this book goes to press—intact, bold, functional, cherished by its users—across Whiskey Row in Prescott, Arizona persists Sam Steiger's/Arizona Department of Transportation's, professionally executed, yellow, midblock, goddam street crossing.

And there it will stay. Until somebody hires a lawyer to remove it.

Selected Reading

Abrahams, Gerald.
Lunatics and Lawyers,
London: Home and Val Thal, 1951

Berger, Bill and Ricardo Martinez.
What to Do With a Dead Lawyer,
Berkeley: Ten Speed Press, 1988.

Bierce, Ambrose.
The Enlarged Devil's Dictionary,
edited by Ernest Jerome Hopkins, Garden City:
Doubleday & Company, Inc., 1967.

Dunne, Finley Peter.
My Dooley on the Choices of Law,
edited by Edward J. Bander, Charlottesville:
The Michie Co., 1963

Jackson, Stanley.
Laughter at Law,
London: Arthur Barker Ltd., 1961.

Shaw, Richard C. and Gregg W. Myers.
Lawyers: Getting Even,
Phoenix: the Pensus Group, unpublished, © 1989.

White, Daniel R.
Trials & Tribulations: Appealing Legal Humor,
Highland Park: Catbird Press, 1989.

Contingency fee law.
Where legal eagles are birds of a different feather.

Recently Forbes blasted America's plaintiff attorneys for their greedy, vulturous ways. And now the tort system, which costs Americans an estimated $80 billion a year in higher insurance bills and court expenses, has come under attack.

No only are contingency fees obscenely high, but one law scholar says they are probably illegal, since contingency fees were created to encourage lawyers to take the poor's risky cases, their legality is highly questionable if there is no realistic risk of damages not being rewarded. Which is the case 95% of the time.

What's more, the standard one-third fee charged by trial lawyers amounts to price-fixing. And if corporations did it, they'd land in court.

Where were the other business magazines while these lawyers were making fortunes off the unfortunate? Treading softly, probably mindful of their vulnerable corporate parents. Which is why only independent Forbes had the guts to tackle this litigious crowd.

—*From an ad placed by* Forbes *Magazine in the May 7, 1990 issue of* Advertising Age.

There's no end to jokes about lawyers...

Feel free to continue your collection here...

_____

_____

_____

_____

_____

_____

_____

_____

_____

_____

_____

_____

_____

Hear a good lawyer joke?
Send it to **Prickly Pear Press** for inclusion
in a possible sequel, *Again, Kill the Lawyers!*

Books Distributed by **Prickly Pear Press:**

A Little War of Our Own: The Pleasant Valley Feud Revisited, by Don Dedera, $14.95 softcover, $21.95 hardcover.

Houseboating on Lake Powell, by Bob Hirsch, $7.95 softcover.

Savvy Sayin's by Ken Alstad, $7.95 softcover.